TRANSPORTATION

YESTERDAY'S SCIENCE
TODAY'S TECHNOLOGY
SCIENCE ACTIVITIES

TRANSPORTATION

ROBERT GARDNER

DRAWINGS BY DORIS ETTLINGER

TFCB

TWENTY-FIRST CENTURY BOOKS

A DIVISION OF HENRY HOLT AND COMPANY / NEW YORK

Twenty-First Century Books
A Division of Henry Holt and Company, Inc.
115 West 18th Street
New York, NY 10011

Henry Holt® and colophon are trademarks of
Henry Holt and Company, Inc.
Publishers since 1866

Library of Congress Cataloging-in-Publication Data
Gardner, Robert, 1929–
Transportation / Robert Gardner.—1st ed.
p.   cm.—(Yesterday's science, today's technology)
Includes index.
1. Transportation—Juvenile literature.   2. Transportation—Experiments—Juvenile literature.
3. Power (Mechanics)—Experiments—Juvenile literature. [1. Transportation—Experiments.
2. Power (Mechanics) Experiments.   3. Experiments.]   I. Title.   II. Series: Gardner, Robert,
1929-   Yesterday's science, today's technology.
TA1149.G37   1994
629.04'078—dc20   94–19409
                                                   CIP
                                                    AC
ISBN 0-8050-2853-6
First edition—1994

Printed in the United States of America
All first editions are printed on acid-free paper ∞.

1   3   5   7   9   10   8   6   4   2

Photo Credits
Cover: © Index Stock Photography
p. 11: © Alaska Division of Tourism; p. 22: © North Wind Picture Archives; p. 35 © The
Bettmann Archive; p. 37; © Japan Railways Group; p. 51: © North Wind Picture Archives;
p. 55: © Exxon U.S.A.; p. 61: © Jim Steinberg/Photo Researchers, Inc.; p. 66: © U.S. Naval
Institute; p. 75: courtesy of the British Tourist Authority.

CONTENTS

INTRODUCTION

Consider a world without cars, trucks, buses, and airplanes. It's difficult to believe, but only a century ago trains and boats were the only means of long-distance travel. Local travel was done on foot, on horseback, or in horse-drawn carriages. Two centuries ago, when our nation was in its infancy, boats were the primary means of traveling great distances. A trip from New York to Boston took several days in good weather. In the early nineteenth century, a "rapid transit" coach traveling the 80 kilometers (50 miles) from Providence, Rhode Island, to Boston, Massachusetts, might make the trip in as little as five hours, but passengers complained of the speed and the bumpy ride. Roads were not paved and in wet weather they became rutted and mud-filled.

Today we can fly around the world in two days and drive from Boston, Massachusetts, to Providence, Rhode Island, in less than an hour. We take for granted the marvels of modern transportation and anticipate even faster modes of transportation in the near future. But our present means of transportation are based on scientific principles and technology that have a long history. Without the wheel, we still would be traveling on foot or on some animal's back.

In this book you'll have an opportunity to investigate some of the science and technology associated with transportation. You'll learn, through reading and in hands-on fashion, some of the basic principles that make transportation possible. Each chapter contains a number of activities designed to enhance your understanding of the subject. You will find an ✖ beside a few of the activities. The ✖ indicates that you should ask an adult to help you because the activity may involve an action or the use of something that might be dangerous. Be sure to find adult help before attempting activities marked in this way.

Some of the activities, which are preceded by a ★, might serve as starting points for a science fair project. Bear in mind, however, that judges at such contests are looking for original ideas and creative thinking. Projects copied from a book are not likely to impress anyone. However, you may find that one or more of the activities in this book will stimulate a project or experiment of your own design that will lead you to the winner's circle at your school's next science or invention fair.

1

WHEELS: A FOUNDATION FOR TRANSPORTATION

Most modes of transportation depend on wheels. Even most boats have wheels in their engines and a steering wheel to turn the rudder. Because wheels are so essential to transportation, this first chapter will focus on this simple piece of technology and its use in the bicycle, a human-powered vehicle that is basically a pair of wheels and a set of pedals.

How Our Ancestors Traveled

Early humans had only one means of transportation—their feet. Later, animals such as donkeys, horses, mules, oxen, reindeer, llamas, elephants, and camels were ridden or used to carry loads from place to place.

Domesticated animals were used to drag boards loaded with stones and other heavy material across the ground. At some point, someone realized the task would be easier if the front ends of their "stone boats" were curved. Still later, the boards were mounted on runners much like the sleds you may use on snow and ice. Such sleds, drawn by dogs, are still used as a means of transporting goods over the snow-covered regions of North America.

While sledges were useful on snow and ice, it was difficult to drag heavily loaded ones across bare ground. Friction between the load and the ground increased as the load grew heavier. To make work easier, heavy loads were often placed on rollers. You'll see why when you do Activity 1.

TO DRAG OR TO ROLL: SLEDGES, ROLLERS, AND FRICTION

MATERIALS
- *wagon large enough for someone to sit in*
- *weight (such as a pail of sand)*
- *spring scale*
- *wooden dowels or metal rollers longer than the wagon's width*

Find a wagon in which you can pull someone. Turn it upside down on a level surface (a concrete floor or walk will do nicely). Place a weight, such as a pail of sand, on the wagon's inverted lower side. Pull the wagon along the level surface with a spring scale. (If you don't have a spring scale, get a feel for the force you apply with your hands and arms.) How much force is needed to move the wagon at a slow but steady speed?

Now, place the inverted wagon and weight on wooden dowels or metal rollers as shown in Figure 1. Be sure you place several rollers in front of the wagon so its front end will be

Dogsledding in Alaska

over new rollers as it moves forward. How much force is required to pull the weighted wagon on the rollers?

Finally, turn the wagon right side up, put the weight in the wagon, and again pull it with the spring balance. How much force is needed to pull the wagon now? Compare the forces needed to move the inverted wagon, the wagon on rollers, and the wagon on wheels. How much do rollers and wheels reduce the friction between the wagon and the surface on which it moves?

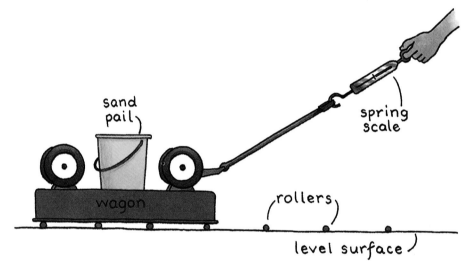

Figure 1. How do rollers change the friction between a heavy weight and the surface over which it moves?

Wheels

No one knows exactly when or by whom the wheel was invented, but it was probably first used about 5,000 years ago in the region near present-day Turkey, Iraq, and Syria. Although it is one of the greatest (and simplest) pieces of technology ever devised, no scientific breakthrough led to its development. Early wheels, as shown in Figure 2a, were often made by fastening three planks together and then cutting them to make a circle. It is known that Roman engineers used strong wheels to move building columns and stones as shown in Figure 2b.

Wheels are everywhere. Just look! Nearly every machine has a wheel of some kind, whether visible or hidden. Normally, we think of wheels as circular objects that roll beneath a vehicle such as a car, truck, train, or wagon. Where else do you find wheels that roll?

Not all wheels roll; some, such as a Ferris wheel or the gears in a clock, simply turn in place without going anywhere. How many wheels can you think of that rotate but don't roll?

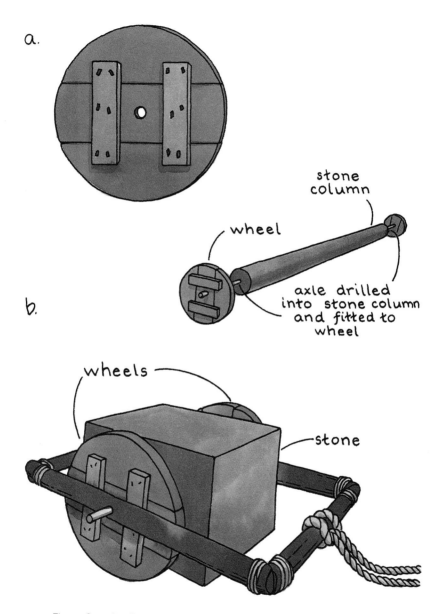

Figure 2: a. A wheel made by fastening three planks together.
b. Wheels were used in Rome to move building columns and
stones.

ROLLING WHEELS

MATERIALS

- *wagon large enough for someone to sit in*
- *tape*
- *drawing compass (or some round objects)*
- *sheet of cardboard*
- *scissors*
- *cylindrical oatmeal box or wooden dowel*
- *paper fasteners or thumbtacks*

The wheels on most vehicles are attached to opposite ends of an axle that connects the wheels. It was true of the wagon you used in Activity 1. But does the axle turn with the wheels, or are the wagon's wheels fastened so they can turn without turning the axle?

Pull your wagon in a circle as shown in Figure 3a. Does the wheel on the outside of the circle go around the same number of times as the wheel on the inside of the circle? To find out, put a piece of tape on the rim of both the inside and outside rear wheels of the wagon. Pull the wagon slowly in a circle. Have a friend count the number of times the outside wheel goes around while you count the rotations of the inside wheel. Which wheel goes around more times? Which wheel goes farther? How does changing the size of the circle change the number of times each wheel turns? Does it make a difference in the ratio:

$$\frac{\text{turns of outside wheel}}{\text{turns of inside wheel}} ?$$

Can you pull the wagon in a circle so that one rear wheel does not rotate at all?

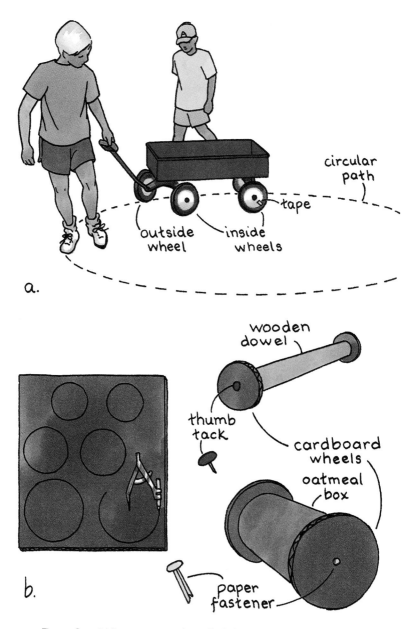

Figure 3: a. When a wagon is pulled along a circular path, do the inside and outside wheels travel the same distance? b. Wheels can be made from cardboard and attached to axles with thumbtacks or paper fasteners.

Use a drawing compass (or some round objects) to draw pairs of different size circles on a sheet of cardboard. Cut out the circles with scissors and attach their centers firmly to an oatmeal box with paper fasteners or to a wooden dowel with thumbtacks (see Figure 3b).

If you give one of your wheels and axle a push, does it move along a straight line or in a circle? Can you explain why?

What happens if you try to make the wheels and axle move in a circle? How can you build a set of wheels firmly fixed to an axle that will move in a circle?

When a car goes around a curve, why do the wheels on the outside of the curve have to rotate faster than those on the inside of the curve? If you look at the underside of a car that is raised on a lift at a garage (with the owner's permission, of course), you can see that the front wheels (on a car with front-wheel drive) are attached to an axle that has a bulge in its middle. (A car with rear-wheel drive has the bulge on the rear axle.) The bulge contains the differential—a set of gears that enables the engine to drive both wheels while allowing one wheel to turn faster than the other. Clearly, the differential, invented by the Chinese in the third century A.D., is an essential part of the modern car.

Old-fashioned railroad cars had axles that turned with the wheels. How did such cars go around curves? Hint: Look at the shape of railroad car wheels shown in Figure 4.

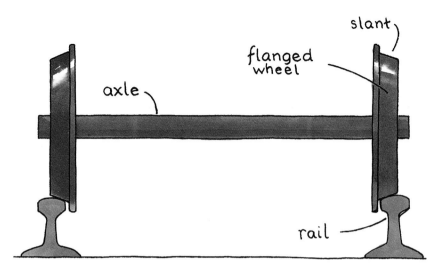

Figure 4. Notice that the flanged wheels of a railroad car are slanted. How would this enable the wheels, which turn with the axles, to go around curves?

ACTIVITY 3

WHEELS AND ODOMETERS

MATERIALS

- *wagon*
- *marking pen*
- *ruler, yardstick, meter stick, or measuring tape*

The odometer on a car or truck tells you how far the vehicle has traveled. A series of gears and a flexible wire connect the meter to a wheel. The gear that measures tenths of a mile is divided into 10 teeth numbered from 0 to 9. When it has gone around once (after one mile), it moves the next gear, which measures miles. This gear, in turn, moves the next gear when it turns once (after 10 miles) and so on until the 10,000-mile-indicating gear is turned. What is the maximum number of miles that can be recorded on most automobile odometers?

How can the number of turns of a wheel measure distance? To find out, make a line with a marking pen on one tire of your wagon where it touches the ground. Make another mark on the ground that is right next to the line on the tire. Pull the wagon forward slowly until the line on the tire indicates that the wheel has made one complete turn. Make a new mark on the ground. How can you find the distance the wagon has moved? How can you find the distance the wagon would move for ten turns of the wheel? How can you find the number of turns of the wheel required to travel one-tenth of a mile? To travel one mile?

Why is the distance that the wagon travels for each turn of the wheel equal to the wheel's circumference? Measure the wheel's diameter. What is the ratio of the wheel's circumference to its diameter? Is this ratio the same for all wheels?

Wheels and Levers: Another Theory

It's possible that wheels were first used not for transporting things but as levers for lifting water from wells. The science of levers was developed by Archimedes (287–212 B.C.), but levers were in use long before Archimedes. The lever is another example of a technology that preceded any scientific explanation of how it works. Activity 4 will help you to understand how wheels can serve as levers.

LEVERS AND WHEELS AS LEVERS

MATERIALS
- *playground seesaw*
- *meter stick or yardstick*
- *bathroom scale*
- *bicycle*
- *weight, such as a brick*
- *strong string*

Find a seesaw that is balanced when set on the fulcrum (bar on which the beam rests) at its midpoint. Sit on one end of the seesaw while someone of about your weight sits on the other end. You'll find that the seesaw remains balanced. But what happens if someone much heavier than you sits opposite you? Where must that person sit to make the seesaw balance? If someone much lighter than you sits on the other end, where must you sit to restore balance?

Archimedes discovered that a lever, such as a seesaw, supported at its midpoint would be balanced if the weight multiplied by its distance from the midpoint was equal for both sides. For example, if a 45-kg (100-lb) person sits 120 cm (4 ft) from the center on one side, the seesaw will balance if a 90-kg (200-lb) person sits 60 cm (2 ft) from the center on the other side. In general:

weight × distance to center = weight × distance to center

With a seesaw, a meter stick or yardstick, and a bathroom scale you can test Archimedes' discovery for yourself. Does it work?

Have a friend sit at one end of a seesaw. Try to lift your friend by pulling down on the opposite end of the seesaw. If you succeed in lifting your friend, lower him or her slowly back to the ground. Don't release the seesaw suddenly! Now have your friend sit closer to the center of the seesaw. Why does the pull you have to exert to lift your friend decrease as he or she moves closer to the center of the seesaw?

To see how a wheel can be used as a lever, turn a bicycle upside down. Attach a string to a weight. Tie the loose end to the inside end of a spoke on the front wheel so that the string will wrap around the axle when the wheel turns. Lift the weight a short way by turning the wheel with your hand on the rim of the wheel. How does the force you have to exert on the rim to lift the weight compare with the actual weight of the object?

Now lift the weight by pulling on a spoke. How does the force you have to exert on the wheel to lift the weight change as you move your hand closer to the wheel's axle? How can a wheel and axle be used as a lever?

By pulling on the inverted bike's pedal you can make the rear wheel go around. Place one hand on a pedal and the other hand on the rim of the back wheel. How does the force you have to exert on the wheel to keep it from turning compare with your force on the pedal? Can you explain why?

Bicycles

The science and technology of the bicycle—wheels, gears, chains, and levers—consisted of principles and materials that had been known and used for years. But no one believed balance was ⸝oss ʾle on a two-wheeled vehicle.

The precursor of the bicycle was the hobbyhorse—a bicycle without pedals or sprockets (wheels with teeth). It was a heavy,

An 1884 bicycle with pedals

wooden-wheeled vehicle with a seat and handlebars attached to the front wheel. A rider straddled the hobbyhorse and pushed it forward with his or her feet. Karl von Drais (1785–1851), who patented the vehicle in 1815, demonstrated that a hobbyhorse rider could exceed walking speeds and even beat horse-drawn wagons over a two-hour journey. The reason was that a person *could achieve balance* on the vehicle, and, by coasting down hills, he or she could easily pass walkers and even horses pulling wagons.

In 1838, Kirkpatrick Macmillan (1810–1878), a Scottish blacksmith, added pedals with connecting rods to the rear wheels. Later, in 1861, Pierre Michaux, a Paris carriage maker, attached the pedals to the front wheels. Michaux was a fine craftsman and promoter who built a factory to mass-produce his velocipedes at a rate of five per day. He held demonstrations and sponsored races to bring his vehicles to the attention of the public.

In the 1870s, James Starley (1830–1881) invented the resilient, steel-spoked wheel shown in Figure 5. In the next decade, his nephew, John Starley, designed a chain-driven bicycle. With the addition of pneumatic tires and ball bearings to reduce friction, by 1900 the bicycle became a safe, comfortable, and reasonably rapid means of transportation. Although improvements in gearing, tires, and lightweight framing continued, the bicycle in 1900 was very similar to those of today.

★ **ACTIVITY 5**

GEARS, OR WHEELS WITH TEETH

MATERIALS
- *multispeed bicycle*
- *two spring balances*

- *string*
- *tape*
- *paper*
- *pencil*

The pedals on a bicycle are attached to the front sprocket, which is connected to the rear sprocket by a chain. In the case of a bike with more than one gear ratio, either the front, the rear, or both sprockets may have more than one geared wheel. For example, a ten-speed bike may have two toothed-wheels on the front sprocket and five on the rear sprocket. How can a

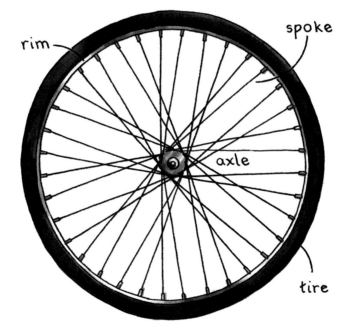

Figure 5. Starley's steel-spoked wheel with radial tangent-tension spoking is still used in bicycles today. Take a look!

rider use any one of ten different connections between front and rear sprockets?

From experience, you probably know that changing gears to make a bike easier to pedal also reduces your speed. To see how changing gears changes both speed and the force you have to exert on the pedals, you can use a bicycle and a pair of spring scales. (If you don't have spring scales, you can probably feel the differences in force with just your hands and arms.)

Turn the bike upside down Use string and tape to tie one spring scale to the rim of the rear wheel and the other to a pedal as shown in Figure 6. Start with the bike in its lowest gear ratio—the one you use to ascend very steep hills. Pull on the pedal while a friend keeps the wheel from turning by pulling against it with the other spring balance. How do the two forces compare? Record your data.

Remove the spring scales and, without changing gears, slowly turn the pedal around once. Have your friend hold the wheel gently and notice how many times the wheel goes around when the pedal makes one turn. How far would the bike travel for each turn of the pedals?

Repeat the experiment using a medium gear ratio (one you might use for a gentle incline) and a high gear ratio (one you would use on a level or declined surface). Record your data for each trial. Which gear ratio (low, medium, or high) allows you to exert the greatest force on the rear wheel? Which ratio makes the bike travel farthest per pedal turn? How does the number of teeth on the rear-sprocket gear affect the number of wheel turns per pedal turn? Can you explain why? What do you think is meant by the terms high, low, and medium gear ratios?

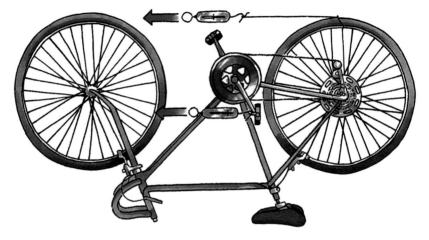

Figure 6. An upside-down bike and spring scales can be used to find how the force applied to the pedal compares with the force applied to the wheel.

BALL BEARINGS

MATERIALS
- *two heavy cans with narrow rims, such as unopened one-gallon cans of paint*
- *5 or 6 marbles of the same diameter*

Fast-turning wheels on vehicles are often mounted on ball bearings. To see why, place a heavy can on a similar can that has a rim around its top. Notice how hard it is to turn the top can. Remove the top can and place 5 or 6 equally spaced marbles so they can roll along the rim at the top of the lower can. Replace the second can on top of the marbles. Again, try turning the upper can. How have the "ball bearings" changed the friction between the two cans? Why are ball bearings used in fast-turning wheels?

2

TRAVELING OVERLAND ON TRAINS AND CARS

You may think that the bicycle, because it is human-powered, is our oldest form of overland vehicle transportation. Actually, transportation by train and bicycle both evolved during the nineteenth century. The automobile, a more recent form of transportation, evolved rapidly during the twentieth century, often replacing more efficient and less polluting public forms of transportation such as light trains and streetcars.

Trains, Steam Engines, Pumps, Gases, and Heat

The steam locomotive pulling a train of cars along parallel rails was the forerunner of today's trains. It was the invention of the steam engine that made such locomotives possible. The steam engine, which led to the industrial revolution as well as to improved modes of transportation, was based on a number of scientific principles discovered during the seventeenth and eighteenth centuries.

Joseph Black (1728–1799) discovered that the heat needed to change water to steam was more than five times the heat needed to raise the temperature of the same weight of water from its freezing point to its boiling point. Robert Boyle's (1627–1691) investigations revealed that the volume of a gas decreases when the pressure on it increases. In fact, he showed that doubling the pressure on an enclosed gas halved its volume—a relationship known as Boyle's law. Jacques Charles (1746–1823) and Guillaume Amontons (1663–1705) both demonstrated that at a fixed pressure the volume of a gas increases uniformly with temperature. Others showed that the pressure exerted by a confined gas increases uniformly with temperature.

✖ ★ **ACTIVITY 7**

GASES, PRESSURE, AND TEMPERATURE

MATERIALS
- *saucepan*
- *stove or hot plate*
- *clock*
- *needleless syringe*
- *narrow-necked glass bottle*
- *clay*
- *transparent or translucent straw*
- *glass of water*
- *washcloth*
- *ice water*
- *clean, empty one-gallon metal can with screw-on cap or rubber stopper that fits its opening*
- *gloves*

You can do one of the experiments that led Black to realize that a lot of heat was needed to change water from a liquid to a gas (steam). Under adult supervision, pour about a cup of water into a saucepan. Place the pan on a stove or hot plate. Record the time when you begin heating the water. How many minutes does it take for the water to reach the boiling point? How long does it take before practically all the water has boiled away? (Be sure to remove the pan before all the water has disappeared!) How does the heat required to change a cup of water to steam compare with the heat needed to warm that water from room temperature to the boiling point?

If you have ever pumped air into a bicycle tire, you have evidence to support Boyle's law. As you squeeze air into the tire, you have to push harder the farther you push the piston. You can demonstrate the same thing in a more visible way by placing your finger over the open end of the cylinder of a needleless, air-filled syringe. Push down on the piston as shown in Figure 7a. What happens when you release the piston?

To see how a gas (air) expands with temperature, cover the mouth of a narrow-necked glass bottle with a piece of clay that has a transparent or translucent straw through its center (see Figure 7b). Be sure there is no open space between the straw and the clay. Turn the bottle over so the straw projects downward into a glass of water. Watch what happens at the end of the straw as you warm the air in the bottle with your hands. How can you explain the bubbles that form?

Next, wrap the bottle with a washcloth that has been soaked in ice water. Why does water move up the straw when you cool the air in the jar?

Ask an adult to help you with this experiment. Pour about half a cup of water into an empty, thoroughly cleaned one-gallon metal can. Heat the can on a hot plate or stove for a few minutes to be certain the can is filled with steam. (When the water boils, it forms steam that replaces the air in the can.) Have the adult, wearing gloves, remove the can from the heat and quickly seal its opening with a screw-on cap or a rubber stopper. Watch the can as it cools and the steam inside condenses. Can you explain why the can collapses?

Figure 7: a. What happens to the volume of an enclosed gas when the pressure on the gas increases? b. What happens to the volume of a gas when its temperature increases?

The Steam Engine

Activity 7 will help you understand how a steam engine works. In the first steam engines (around 1700), a piston was pushed in one direction by the pressure of steam entering a cylinder. To make the piston return to its original position, the cylinder was sprayed with cold water to make the steam condense. As the steam condensed, the pressure in the cylinder decreased, and air pressure on the other side of the piston forced it back to its original position.

By the end of the eighteenth century, James Watt (1736–1819) had developed a steam engine similar to the one shown in Figure 8. Refer to this figure as you read the next two paragraphs.

Watt, who was familiar with Black's work, realized that considerable fuel was wasted every time the cylinder had to be reheated after being cooled to reduce the pressure. To avoid this, Watt cooled the steam in a condenser outside the cylinder. He also developed moving valves that allowed steam to push the piston back and forth. As one valve opened to allow steam to enter one side of the cylinder, a valve on the other side closed off incoming steam and opened a pipe that carried spent steam to the condenser. The

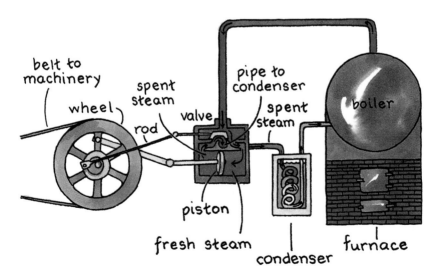

Figure 8. Watt's engine used steam to drive a piston both right and left. A pipe carried spent steam to a condenser and from there back to the boiler. By separating the condenser from the cylinder, Watt's engine used about one-third as much fuel as older ones.

pressure of the steam connected to the condenser quickly dropped as it cooled and was forced out of the cylinder by the steam pushing on the other side of the piston.

Watt used a rod to connect the piston to a wheel that moved the valves back and forth. The wheel, in turn, was connected by a belt or gears to machines that might turn factory or farm machinery, a riverboat's water wheel, or the wheels of a locomotive.

Later, the advent of steel-plated boilers allowed engineers to use steam under much higher pressure. This led to more efficient multicylinder steam engines. After driving one piston, the pressure of the expanded steam was still sufficient to drive one or more additional pistons before reaching the condenser.

Steam Engines, Trains, Rails, and Transportation

In 1808, a steam locomotive was used to pull passengers in a carriage around a small circular track in London. Although this first railroad was little more than a form of public entertainment, the next half century saw rail transportation spread across England.

In the United States, railroads offered a means of transportation across the vast lands of a new and expanding country. By 1838 there were 350 locomotives pulling cars along 2,400 km (1,500 mi) of iron tracks. At the beginning of the Civil War the system had grown to 48,000 km (30,000 mi) of tracks. Forty years later, nearly 2,000 trains moved freight and passengers along 320,000 km (200,000 mi) of rails linking cities on the Atlantic Ocean with those along the Pacific Ocean.

As the twentieth century began, power companies were generating electrical energy and sending it along wires to distant homes and factories. The availability of electrical energy led to light trains, trolleys, and streetcars powered by electric motors connected to overhead power lines. Electrically powered vehicles became a popular means of transportation in cities before World War II. After the war, the rapid growth of buses and automobile traffic led to the

An 1875 steam locomotive

demise of streetcars in most American cities, although subways still flourished.

During the 1930s, diesel-powered locomotives began to replace steam engines on the railroads. They were much cleaner and more efficient than the coal-burning steam locomotives.

Tomorrow's Trains

Although trains still pull freight and carry commuters to and from work, long-distance travelers today generally fly. However, crowded airports and a new technology may soon provide a boost for trains as a means of transportation. The new technology involves maglev trains, which are being developed in Japan and Germany.

Maglev is an abbreviation for magnetic levitation—a system that uses magnetic forces to lift a train so that it floats on air. A coil of wire carrying an electric current acts like a magnet. A changing magnetic field can generate an electric current in a coil of wire. These principles are used in building a maglev train. In Japan, superconductors (materials that offer no resistance to the flow of electricity) are used in the electromagnets on the maglev trains. These electromagnets induce electric currents in the aluminum coils within the guideway's floor as shown in Figure 9a. The repulsion between the two magnets lifts the train off the guideway. Because superconductors work only at very low temperatures, Japanese engineers have had to use expensive liquid helium to cool the superconductors in the train. Recent research has led to the development of materials that become superconductors at a higher temperature, the temperature of liquid nitrogen, which is much less expensive. This breakthrough should reduce the cost and speed the development of maglev trains in Japan.

Germany's maglev train uses powerful conventional electromagnets to create attractive forces that lift the train above the guideway as shown in Figure 9b. In both systems, the train is alternately pulled and pushed forward by changing the direction of the magnetic fields as shown in Figure 9c.

Maglev trains are relatively inexpensive to build, require only a narrow path of land, and provide a nearly silent, pollution-free ride. Furthermore, the vehicle wraps around the guideway and can't be derailed. Because future maglevs will travel at speeds as high as 480 km/hr (300 mi/hr), they have the potential to revolutionize transportation over distances up to 800 km (500 mi). (Air travel is more economical over longer distances.) In the United States, they will be used to move people between airports and cities, to provide rapid transport within cities, and to connect cities that are separated by 800 km (500 mi) or less.

A modern maglev train

36

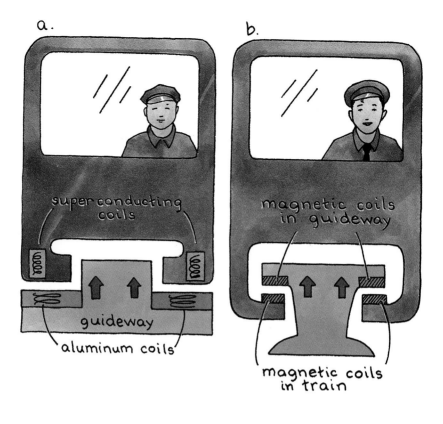

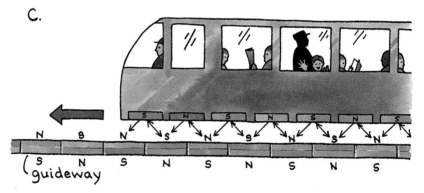

Figure 9: a. The Japanese maglev train is lifted off the guideway by magnetic repulsion. b. The German maglev train is lifted off the guideway by magnetic attraction. c. The polarity of the guideway magnets is switched so that they alternately pull and push the train forward.

LEVITATING MAGNETS

MATERIALS

■ *several ceramic ring magnets, which have holes through their centers (These can be purchased at stores that sell electronic supplies.)*

■ *pencil or soda straw*

To see how a maglev train works, place a pair of ceramic ring magnets on a pencil or soda straw. Turn the magnets so that their like poles (north-north or south-south) repel each other. Notice how the upper magnet "floats" on the lower one. This is the same principle that lifts a maglev train off the guideway.

Have a friend gently support the pencil or straw while you move a third magnet near the one that is floating. The upper magnet represents the maglev train. Can you pull it forward by attracting it with the magnet in your hand? Can you push it forward by repelling it with the magnet in your hand?

Computerized PRT

For some urban areas, PRT (personal rapid transit) may be the main form of intracity transportation in the twenty-first century. As envisioned by Boston University professor of engineering Edward Anderson, PRT will consist of hundreds of small (two or three passenger), electrically powered vehicles moving along a lightweight, elevated track. As a passenger, you will use a credit card to both enter a terminal and pay the fare. After entering, you will press a series of keys on a computer to indicate your destination. The computer will direct you to the proper track and indicate the number of the car you should take. Once you enter the car and close the door, it is programmed to carry you to your destination along the shortest route.

The Automobile: King of the Road

The first automobiles were called horseless carriages, and rightly so because they were little more than a carriage with an engine. Many of the first automobiles, which appeared shortly before 1900, were powered by steam or electricity. In fact, the first automobile to travel faster than a train was a Stanley Steamer. It achieved a speed of 240 km/hr (150 mi/hr) in 1907, but steam cars never gained wide acceptance. They were noisy, and people were afraid of the hot steam and the open flame required to heat the boiler. In the winter vast clouds of white smoke formed when the car was in use, and the water froze when it was not in use.

Between 1900 and 1912, more than 100 companies made electric cars. They were very quiet and easy to drive and operate, but they were slow and had a limited range because the batteries had to be recharged frequently. In rural areas of the United States around 1900, few towns had electric power. Consequently, electric cars were impractical because there was no convenient way to recharge their batteries.

Because of the problems associated with steam and electric cars, those powered by internal combustion engines, particularly the gasoline engine, soon became the most popular. In a steam engine, the fuel is burned outside the cylinder; in an internal combustion engine, the fuel, mixed with air, is burned within the cylinder. Usually it is ignited by a spark. In the case of diesel engines, the pressure within the cylinder becomes so large that the increased temperature is enough to ignite the fuel. In either case, the fuel burns so fast that it is really an explosion. The rise in temperature causes the gases to expand and increase in pressure, driving the piston along the cylinder as shown in Figure 10.

Étienne Lenoir (1822–1900), a French engineer, built the first successful internal combustion engine in 1859. His design, based on theoretical studies of heat engines done by Nicolas Carnot (1753–1823), used an induction coil to make a spark that ignited a mixture of air and coal gas within a cylinder. The exploding gases

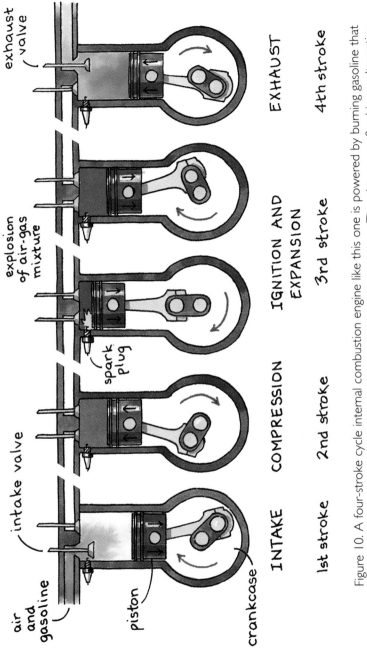

exhaust valve

explosion of air-gas mixture

spark plug

intake valve

air and gasoline

piston

crankcase

INTAKE
1st stroke

COMPRESSION
2nd stroke

IGNITION AND EXPANSION
3rd stroke

EXHAUST
4th stroke

Figure 10. A four-stroke cycle internal combustion engine like this one is powered by burning gasoline that is ignited by a spark. Most gasoline engines contain several cylinders. The pistons are fired in an alternating fashion so that the crankshaft turns smoothly.

drove a piston in the cylinder. In 1860, Lenoir built the first horseless carriage when he used his engine to turn the wheels of a wagon.

Additional theoretical studies showed that Lenoir's engine could be made more efficient if the gas were compressed before it was ignited and if there were more than one stroke in the engine's cycle. These studies led Nikolaus Otto (1832–1891), in Germany, to build a four-stroke cycle gasoline engine, which he patented in 1876. His engine was similar to the one shown in Figure 10.

By 1900, Carl Benz (1844–1929) and Gottlieb Daimler (1834–1900) had built horseless carriages powered by Otto's engine. In fact, all the essential features of today's gasoline-powered automobile were developed by this time.

The task of Benz and Daimler and other early car builders was to connect the engine's flywheel at the end of its crankshaft to the wheels of a vehicle. They did this by means of a clutch, a gearbox, and a mechanical link between the gearbox and the wheels, as shown in Figure 11.

A clutch consists of two plates, one attached to the flywheel, the other to the main shaft of the gearbox. A pedal is used to engage and disengage the clutch. When the clutch is disengaged, the motor can run without moving the car. By having several gears in the gearbox, the car, like a bicycle with several gears, can run at different speeds and ascend steep hills. A rotating drive shaft extends from the gearbox to the rear axle where gears and a differential turn the wheels.

A revolution in transportation occurred when Henry Ford (1863–1947) developed a system of mass-producing relatively inexpensive cars. Ford's Model T, which first appeared in 1908, sold for $825. It was the first of 15 million such cars manufactured between 1908 and 1927. This simple but very practical vehicle was soon in great demand. To meet that demand, Ford developed an assembly-line process. Each line put together the 5,000 separate, interchangeable parts to produce a car every 1 hour, 33 minutes.

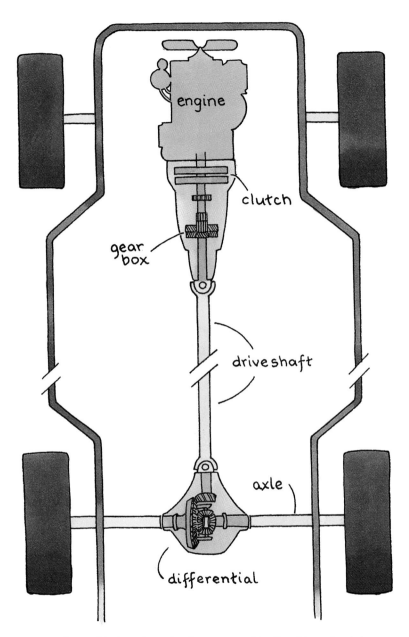

Figure 11. A car's engine is connected to the drive wheels by a clutch and various gears. In many cars today the front wheels are the drive wheels.

After introducing the assembly-line system, Model T production reached nearly a quarter million per year as its price fell to a low of $290 in 1924.

Such affordable cars led many American families to buy them. Between 1910 and 1920 the United States' population grew from 92 million to 106 million, but the number of cars increased almost twenty-fold, from 470,000 to more than 9 million. The widespread and rapid acceptance and use of automobiles forced legislators to provide funding for the construction of roads. Between 1921 and 1951 highway mileage in the United States grew from 619,200 km (387,000 mi) to 1,920,000 km (1,200,000 mi).

By 1990, automobiles dominated American transportation. The nation's nearly 200 million motor vehicles traveled more than 3.2 trillion km (2 trillion mi), far exceeding our use of any other form of transportation. Airlines, for example, covered less than 4 percent as many miles, trains less than 1 percent as many. Even in urban areas, less than 5 percent of the passengers use public transportation. More than 80 percent use automobiles.

★ **ACTIVITY 9**

BRAKES, CARS, HILLS, AND FRICTION

MATERIALS
- *a toy car with wheels that turn freely*
- *long, wide board*
- *two strong rubber bands*
- *ruler*

Before 1920, most automobiles had brakes on the rear wheels only. Such a system created a hazard on slippery hills. To see why, place a toy car with wheels that turn freely on a long, wide board. When you lift the board, the car will roll down the "hill." How high do you have to lift one end of the board before the car rolls?

Place two strong rubber bands across both the front and rear wheels so they cannot turn. The rubber bands serve as brakes on the wheels. How high do you have to lift the end of the board now before the car moves down the hill? How can you account for the difference?

Repeat the experiment, but this time put brakes on only the rear wheels—leave the front wheels so they can turn. What happens when the car starts down the hill? What happens if the car descends with brakes on only its front wheels and with the rear wheels free to turn? Why was it hazardous to have brakes on the rear wheels? Would it have been safer if the brakes had been on the front wheels?

★ **ACTIVITY 10**

CARS AND SAFETY BELTS

MATERIALS
- *large toy car or truck*
- *long, wide board*
- *small toy doll*
- *brick or similar barrier*
- *strong rubber band*

Place a large toy car or truck near one end of a long, wide board. Slowly raise the end of the board next to the car or truck. The toy vehicle will roll down the hill.

Place a "passenger" on your car. (A small toy doll will serve nicely.) Let the car with passenger roll down the hill a few times to be sure the passenger doesn't fall off during the downhill trip. Next, place a barrier, such as a brick, about two car lengths from the bottom of the hill so that the car with passenger will crash into it. What happens to the passenger during the crash?

Finally, use a "safety belt" to fasten the passenger to the vehicle. A strong rubber band can serve as the safety belt. Again, let the car roll down the hill and crash into the barrier. What happens to the passenger this time? How does this experiment show that safety belts can reduce the chances of death or serious injury during an automobile accident?

MEASURING SPEED

MATERIALS
- *measuring tape*
- *wooden stakes*
- *stopwatch*
- *pocket calculator (optional)*
- *paper*
- *pencil*

One of the major causes of automobile accidents is excessive speed. If you're in a car, you can determine the speed by looking at the speedometer. Police sometimes use a speed "gun" (radar) to determine a car's speed, but there is another way. All you need to do is measure the time it takes a car to travel a known distance.

Ask an adult to help you place two stakes next to a highway. The stakes should be several hundred feet apart. Ask a friend to stand away from the road but directly in line with the first stake. Tell your friend to raise his or her hand at the moment an approaching car reaches that stake. At your friend's signal, you can start a stopwatch as you stand in line with the second stake. When the car reaches the second stake, stop the watch. Knowing the distance between the stakes and the time for the car to travel that distance, how can you determine the car's speed in feet per second? In miles per hour?

The Cars of Tomorrow

If physicists and engineers find ways to control the fusion of hydrogen, which can release vast amounts of energy, electric power will become relatively inexpensive. In that event, it's likely that battery-powered electric motors will replace internal combustion engines in cars, particularly as oil supplies diminish. New, improved batteries will provide more electric energy and extend the range of electric cars so they can be driven farther before the batteries need recharging.

Regardless of the energy used to power cars, their bodies will probably be made of flexible plastics and composites that will spring back to their original shape if bent, and their computer-controlled engines will be made of ceramics.

Safety features will include a radar-controlled avoidance system that will automatically brake the vehicle if it moves too close to the one ahead of it and a light system to make the car's speed visible above the hood. A computerized mapping system linked to communications satellites will indicate the car's position on a dashboard map. At the press of a button, a lost motorist will be directed by the computer's voice to whatever destination he or she names.

3

TRAVELING ALONG RIVERS, LAKES, AND OCEANS IN BOATS

The American colonies developed along the Atlantic coast because the only way to come to America was by boat. Once here, boats were the primary means of transporting goods and people over long distances. Rivers, such as the Connecticut, the Delaware, the Hudson, the James, the Potomac, the Savannah, the Susquehanna, and others, carried boats inland, while the Atlantic Ocean provided a pathway between the colonies' ocean ports.

Early Boats

Probably the earliest "boat" was a log floating down the river with someone astride it. Later, logs were fastened together to make rafts that could be used to transport people and goods downriver. Archaeologists have found dugout canoes—large logs that were hollowed out with axes—that are about 10,000 years old. These boats, propelled by paddles, could move upstream as well as downstream.

Egyptians were using sailboats 5,000 years ago; however, these ships could only sail with or at a slight angle to the wind. Moveable, triangular sails that allowed ships to sail into or across the wind were not invented until about 400 A.D. Often, early boats carried oarsmen as well as sails. In the absence of a proper wind, oarsmen provided the force to move the boat. Some seventeenth-century European galleys had as many as 56 oars with five men pulling each oar.

Viking sailors used an oar at the rear, right-hand side of the boat to steer the vessel. This "steerboard" became the origin of the word *starboard,* which means the right side of a boat. Because of the steering oar's location, Viking ships always docked with the left side of the vessel facing port. Hence, port came to mean the left side of a ship.

As early as 1787, John Fitch (1743–1798) used a steam engine to move six long paddles on each side of a boat. However, Fitch's boat was so filled with machinery that it left little room for passengers or freight. But in 1807 Robert Fulton's (1765–1815) steam-powered ship *Clermont* proved to be a profitable venture by transporting passengers between New York City and Albany, New York. It made the 240-km (150-mi) voyage along the Hudson River in 32 hours—three times faster than sailing ships.

The *Clermont's* steam engine was connected to a paddle wheel on the ship's side. The wheel propelled the ship forward. Similar ships still operate on the Mississippi River.

Fulton's first steamboat also had sails.

SINK OR FLOAT AND ARCHIMEDES' PRINCIPLE

MATERIALS

- *sensitive spring scale or a laboratory balance*
- *wooden block*
- *ruler*
- *measuring cup, pint size*
- *water*
- *straight pins*
- *clay or plasticene*
- *empty tuna fish can*
- *pan of water*

People built and used boats for centuries before Archimedes explained why boats float in water. You can rediscover Archimedes' principle by doing the following experiment.

Use a sensitive spring scale or a balance to weigh a wooden block. Then find the volume of the block by multiplying its length by its width by its height. You can also find the block's volume by placing it in a measuring cup partially filled with water. A cup of water has a volume of about 240 mL (8 oz). Push the block beneath the water with a pair of pins. The change of the water level in the measuring cup will indicate the block's volume—the volume of water displaced by the block. How much does the block weigh? What is the block's volume?

When the block is placed in water it floats. What is the weight of the water displaced by the floating block? To find out, first measure the change in the water level in the cup when the block is placed on the water. Then weigh the volume of water displaced. To do this, first weigh the empty measuring cup. Then fill it until it contains the volume of water displaced by the block. Reweigh the partially filled cup and subtract the weight of the empty cup to find the weight of the water displaced. How does the weight of the water displaced by the block compare with the weight of the block?

Repeat the experiment with a ball of clay. Weigh the clay in air and again when it is submerged in water as shown in Figure 12. Record your results and also the weight and volume of the water displaced by the clay. How does the weight of the clay compare with the weight of the water displaced by the clay? How does the clay's loss of weight in water compare with the weight of the water it displaces?

If you measured carefully, you found, as Archimedes did, that any object in water is buoyed upward by a force equal to the weight of the water it displaces. In other words, the weight lost by an object when placed in water is equal to the weight of the water it displaces. The wood block displaced its own weight

Figure 12. Clay can be weighed in air and while submerged in water as shown here. Either a spring scale or a balance can be used.

of water before its top surface reached water level. On the other hand, the clay sank; its weight was greater than the weight of the water it displaced. If you had equal volumes of water, wood, and clay, which would weigh the most? The least?

Using what you have learned, change the shape of the clay ball so that it will float in water. What did you do to make it float? When the clay was a solid lump, it sank in water; now it floats. Why?

Archimedes knew, as you do, that metals would float in water. You can demonstrate that this is true by placing an empty tuna fish can in a pan of water. Why did no one build metal boats for another 2,000 years after Archimedes had discovered it was possible?

Toward Modern Ships

Three engineering advances during the nineteenth century led to the world's first modern passenger ship—*Mauretania*. The vessel was almost 240 meters (800 ft) long and carried 2,335 passengers and a crew of 812 across the Atlantic in five days in 1907. The first advance was building ships of metal. Because metal was much stronger than wood, metal ships could be made larger and lighter than those built of wood. The second advance was the propeller. It was more efficient and moved ships more rapidly than paddle wheels. Finally, the steam turbine joined to a high-pressure boiler easily converted the energy stored in fuel into the kinetic (motion) energy of a rotating propeller.

Metal ships were slow to gain favor among shipbuilders. However, as more and more iron ships survived violent storms that wrecked those made of wood, it became apparent that metal ships were safer and better able to withstand punishment on the high seas and to survive groundings. Furthermore, ships made from iron plates joined with rivets were not only stronger but less expensive to build than wooden vessels. Finally, the larger, longer-lived metal ships could carry more passengers and cargo, making them more profitable to owners than competing wooden vessels.

Although Leonardo da Vinci (1452–1519) had designed a propeller in the fifteenth century, it was not until 1802 that inventor John Stevens (1749–1838) installed a steam-powered propeller on a boat. Propellers, mounted on a ship's bottom at its stern, were more efficient than paddle wheels, particularly in rough seas where side-mounted paddle wheels were often out of the water. In addition, paddle wheels were more exposed to enemy fire than underwater propellers during a naval battle.

In 1894, Sir Charles Parsons (1854–1931), who had designed a steam turbine to drive electric generators in power stations, designed a similar machine for his own 44-ton ship, *Turbinia*. Figure 13a shows a steam-powered turbine. In an electric power plant, the shaft turns a generator; in a ship the shaft is connected to one or more propellers. The propellers, as you can see in Figure 13b, push water backwards.

How can the third law of motion be used to explain the way a rudder or "steerboard" is used to steer a boat?

A modern tanker ready to take on thousands of gallons of oil

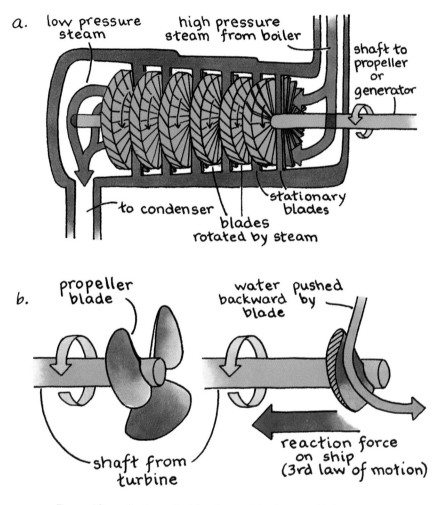

a.
low pressure steam

high pressure steam from boiler

shaft to propeller or generator

to condenser

blades rotated by steam

stationary blades

b.
propeller blade

water pushed backward by blade

shaft from turbine

reaction force on ship (3rd law of motion)

Figure 13: a. A steam turbine is used to turn a ship's propellers as well as the electric generators in power plants. b. A rotating propeller pushes water backwards in order to move the boat forward.

FROM TURBINES AND PROPELLERS
TO PINWHEELS AND FANS

MATERIALS
- *toy pinwheel on a stick*
- *electric fan*

A toy pinwheel can be used as a model of a steam turbine. The blades of the pinwheel represent the blades of a turbine. Air that you blow onto the pinwheel represents the high-pressure steam that pushes on the turbine blades. What happens when you blow air against the pinwheel blades? How does the shape of the pinwheel blades influence the way they move?

A shaft connected to a turbine can be used to turn a propeller. If you've ever ridden in a speedboat, you've seen how the propeller blades push water backwards. This makes the boat move forward. A similar effect can be seen with a fan that blows air. Ask an adult to help you. Before the fan is connected to an electrical outlet, notice the shape of the blades. They are the fan's propellers. Ask the adult to plug in the fan, turn it on for a moment so that it begins to spin, then turn it off. As the fan slows down, notice in which direction the blades turn. Disconnect the fan and examine the blades carefully. Do you see how the blades push air as they turn?

4

TRAVELING THROUGH THE AIR IN BALLOONS AND AIRPLANES

Successful airplane technology followed shortly after Benz and Daimler introduced the automobile. Although the automobile preceded the airplane, changes in airplane technology have been more dramatic. The automobile is still usually powered by a gasoline engine, its size has not changed significantly, and its cruising speed has increased by less than ten times. Meanwhile, airplane engines have changed extensively, their speeds have increased 100-fold (1,000-fold if we include the space shuttle and other rocket-powered vehicles), they carry hundreds of times more passengers, and they have become a far safer means of transportation than the automobile.

Lighter-Than-Air Vehicles

For centuries, humans dreamed of flying like birds. But trying to flap birdlike wings never worked, even when covered with feathers taken from real birds. Most birds, unlike humans, are well adapted for flying. They have light, hollow bones and chest muscles that are very large and strong relative to their body size. These are the muscles that move their wings. Their feathers, which can be turned, capture air and increase the pressure beneath the wings on the downstroke, but turn when the wings rise to offer far less air resistance.

Hot air balloons were first designed by the Montgolfier brothers, Joseph (1740–1810) and Jacques (1745–1799). They filled a large linen bag with hot air and found, as Archimedes would have predicted, that it ascended. An object in air, like one in water, is buoyed upward by a force equal to the weight of the air it displaces. Since a bag filled with hot air weighs less than an equal volume of the cold air that surrounds it, it is pushed upward. If the bag and hot air together weigh less than the buoyant force, the bag will ascend.

The first successful human flight in a hot air balloon carried Jean-François Pilâtre de Rozier (1756–1785) and the Marquis François-Laurent d'Arlandes into the sky above Paris on November 21, 1783. Ten days later, Jacques Charles and a companion traveled 43 km (27 mi) in two and a half hours in a gondola suspended from a hydrogen-filled balloon. Charles realized that the air in a hot air balloon would have to be heated periodically; otherwise, it would descend as the air cooled. A sealed hydrogen balloon, on the other hand, would remain aloft for as long as the pilot desired because the weight of hydrogen was $\frac{1}{14}$ that of an equal volume of air.

Although balloon rides are fun and provide a grand view of the countryside, they are not a good means of transportation because they move only with the wind. Count Ferdinand von Zeppelin (1838–1917) developed satisfactory lighter-than-air ships by building a balloon around a light aluminum frame. Propellers, powered by internal combustion engines, enabled these dirigibles, or zeppelins, to move in any direction.

In 1936 Germany built the 245-m (804-ft) *Hindenburg*. The airship carried 72 passengers who enjoyed hot and cold running water, a dining room and lounge with a grand piano, and promenade decks during a two-day flight from Germany to New Jersey. In 14 months it made 63 flights, including 37 across the Atlantic.

Hot air balloons at a ballooning rodeo in Colorado

Then, on May 6, 1937, as it prepared to moor at Lakehurst, New Jersey, the hydrogen-filled ship burst into flames, killing 36 people.

The *Hindenburg* disaster marked the demise of dirigible transportation. A few dirigibles, such as the Goodyear Blimp, still exist, but they are used mostly for advertising and for positioning television cameras. Even if filled with a nonflammable gas such as helium, they are too slow to compete with modern airplanes or even oceangoing ships.

A HELIUM BALLOON

MATERIALS

- *helium-filled balloon or mylar bag such as those used to convey birthday greetings*
- *long ribbon, heavy string, or twistie*
- *paper clips*

If you release a recently filled helium balloon or bag, it rises to the ceiling. Outdoors it will rise and be carried away by the wind, so be careful. To find out how much "cargo" such a balloon might carry, you can use a long ribbon, heavy string, or a twistie to attach paper clips to the balloon. How many paper clips or what length of ribbon or string can the balloon lift? Can you add just enough weight to make the balloon float so that it neither rises nor sinks? Why does a helium balloon eventually lose its lighter-than-air quality?

The Airplane—A Dream Come True

On December 17, 1903, Orville (1871–1948) and Wilbur (1867–1912) Wright took turns making the first human flights in an airplane—a winged, heavier-than-air, engine-powered vehicle. Their flight times ranged between 12 and 59 seconds as they traveled through the air for distances of 36 to 260 m (120 to 852 ft).

Their success confirmed scientific studies that indicated human flight in heavier-than-air vehicles was possible. The first studies were conducted by George Cayley (1773–1857), an Englishman, who investigated the movement of various types of wings through air. He realized that a light engine was needed to move the winged machine fast enough to provide the necessary lift and to overcome the drag forces that oppose motion. It was Cayley, too, who discovered that the lifting force on the wing depended on the angle at which it struck the air. Aware that steam engines were too heavy to serve as a source of power, he anticipated the internal combustion engine by suggesting that a light engine might be driven by the combustion of inflammable substances.

Lacking the proper engine, Cayley concentrated on building heavier-than-air gliders. In 1853 the eighty-year-old inventor persuaded his coachman to fly the glider from a hilltop. Apparently, the flight was successful because the frightened coachman refused to fly again.

In the 1890s, during some 2,000 flights in Germany, Otto Lilienthal (1848–1896) demonstrated that gliders could generate sufficient lift to carry his body through the air for sustained periods of time. Lilienthal's death following a crash during one of his flights did not deter the Wright brothers, who conducted their own glider flights in 1900 and 1901.

Disappointed by their results, the brothers built a wind tunnel in their Dayton, Ohio, bicycle shop and conducted extensive tests on various wing designs. By 1902, based on their experiments, they tested a new glider design that proved satisfactory and began working on a light engine to provide power for sustained flight. The 80-kg (180-lb) engine they built was connected by bicycle chains to two propellers mounted between the wings of their biplane. The propellers provided the thrust needed to lift the airplane over the beaches near Kitty Hawk, North Carolina, on that historic day in 1903. By 1905, the Wright brothers had become experienced pilots and were making half-hour flights over distances of 32 km (20 mi) in an improved version of their original test plane.

The Science of Flight

The detailed behavior of the air flow around a wing is very complicated. Basically, however, the force needed to lift an airplane can be explained by Newton's third law of motion: when one body exerts a force on another, the second body exerts an equal but opposite force on the first. As air strikes a fast-moving wing, it is deflected downward as shown in Figure 14. The downward force on the air causes an equal upward force on the wing. When a plane takes off, the spinning propeller pushes air backwards just as a boat propeller pushes water. The air, in turn, exerts an equal force forward on the propeller and the plane to which it is attached. The plane builds up speed until the force on the wings due to the deflected air is enough to lift the airplane.

Once in the air and flying at a steady speed, the forces of lift on the wings and the forward thrust due to the propeller balance the weight and drag (air friction) as shown in Figure 15a. The rudder and elevators on the tail together with the wing's ailerons allow the pilot to control the plane (see Figure 15b). An airplane is capable of three basic movements—yaw, pitch, and roll, as shown in Figure 15c.

To make the plane dive, the pilot lowers the elevators. This raises the tail and the nose drops (see Figure 16a). Raising the elevators will make the plane climb. To yaw to the right, the rudder, like

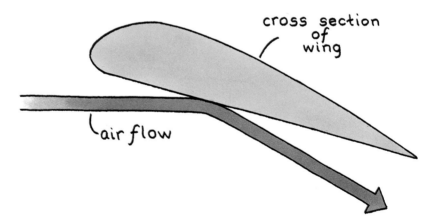

Figure 14. Air deflected downward by the wings gives rise to the reaction force (lift) needed to overcome an airplane's weight.

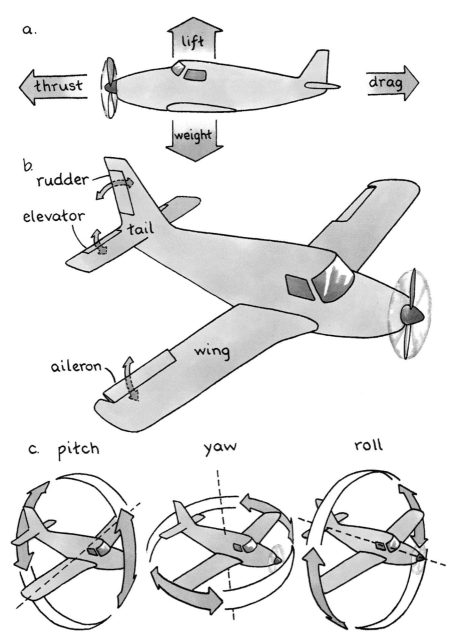

Figure 15: a. In level flight at constant speed, thrust equals drag and lift equals weight. b. A tail rudder and elevators as well as wing ailerons allow a pilot to control the airplane. c. There are three basic movements of an airplane that cause it to change direction. The dotted lines mark axes about which rotation (arrows) occurs. Diving or climbing involve pitch; a right or left turn involves yaw; banking the plane involves roll.

the rudder on a boat, is turned toward the right side of the plane as shown in Figure 16b. The increased deflection of the air to the right pushes the plane's tail to the left, just as water pushes a boat's stern to the left. The plane's nose, therefore, turns right. Lowering the right aileron while raising the left one will lift the plane's right wing and lower its left, as you can see in Figure 16c. Can you explain why? Of course, various combinations of rudder, elevator, and aileron movement can produce complex maneuvers. On large airliners, a variety of flaps on the front and rear of the wings are used to change the size of the wings and to increase or decrease drag and lift, particularly during takeoff and landing.

Helicopters use long rotating blades to drive air downward and, thereby, lift the craft. Once it has attained altitude, the angle of the blades can be changed so that the air is deflected backward as well as downward. This will give the helicopter thrust as well as lift.

Today's Navy helicopters are often used in search and rescue missions.

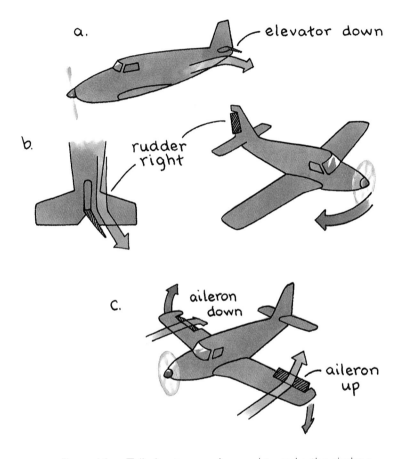

Figure 16: a. Tail elevators are lowered to make the airplane dive or raised to make the plane climb. b. If the rudder is turned to the right, the plane yaws right. c. Raising the left aileron and lowering the right one will make the plane roll to the left.

DESIGNING PAPER AIRPLANES

MATERIALS
- *sheets of paper*
- *paper clips*
- *tape*

Paper airplanes are really paper gliders unless they have some means of propulsion, which most don't have. Nevertheless, you can learn a lot about how airplanes fly by designing and flying paper gliders.

One common design for making a paper glider is shown in Figure 17. Begin by folding an 8½-by-11-inch sheet of paper in half (1). Make a triangular fold outward and downward on each side (2). Make two more folds on each side (3 and 4). Use a piece of clear tape to hold the wings and fuselage in place and your glider is ready to fly.

Additional folds can be made to give your glider ailerons and a rudder. How can these be used to control the flight of your glider? You might also like to add a more extensive tail and a paper clip to change your glider's weight distribution. How can they be used to further control your glider's flight path? How do these various additions affect the forces of lift, drag, and weight acting on your glider?

Does the weight of the paper affect the flight of your glider? To find out, build the glider from two or three sheets of paper instead of one. What do you find?

Does the ratio of weight to surface area affect the flight of your glider? How can you find out?

You might also like to try one or more of the designs in Figure 18, or you may prefer to design your own glider. Can you make one that flies better than any shown here? If you can, how do you explain your success?

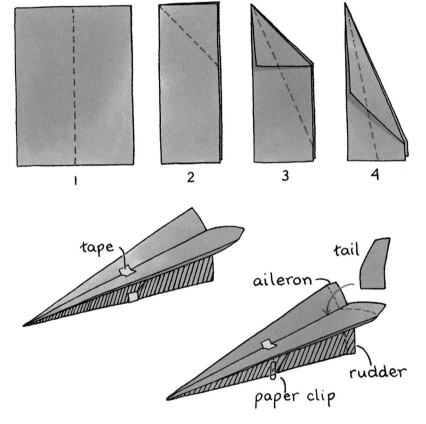

Figure 17. One common design for a paper glider

The Flying Rings

The Conical Glider

The Stubby Flyer

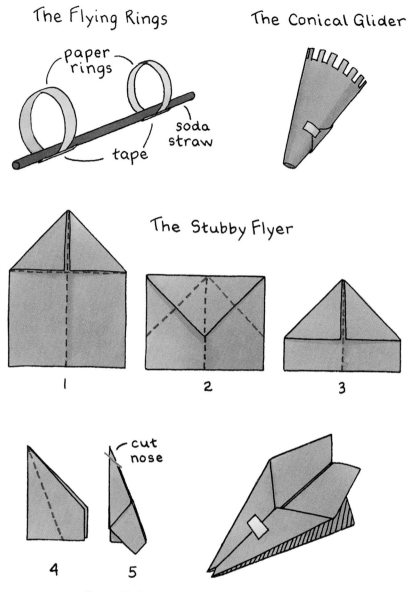

paper rings

soda straw

tape

1

2

3

cut nose

4

5

Figure 18. Other designs for paper gliders

A TOY AIRPLANE

MATERIALS
■ *toy airplane with a rubber-band-powered propeller*

Paper gliders have no way to develop thrust once they leave your hand. Small airplanes have propellers to provide thrust. At a toy store or a hobby shop you can probably find a light toy airplane that has a propeller powered by a wound-up rubber band. Compare the flight of this plane with your paper gliders.

You can increase the plane's weight by adding paper clips or by using thicker wood. How does the plane's weight affect its flight?

If possible, buy some balsa wood and make wings and tails that are smaller and larger than those of the plane you bought. Substitute these homemade structures for the ones in the plane. How does wing and tail size affect the plane's flight? How does their shape affect its flight? How does the position of the wing affect flight? Find a stronger or a weaker rubber band than the one that came with the plane. How does the strength of the rubber band affect the plane's flight? Can you build a plane that flies better than the one you bought?

Airplanes Today

The airplanes used by major airlines today are powered by jet engines that have made worldwide travel common and affordable. A large fan at the front of a jet engine draws in air as shown in Figure 19. The air is then compressed before entering the combustion chamber where it is heated by burning kerosene to further increase

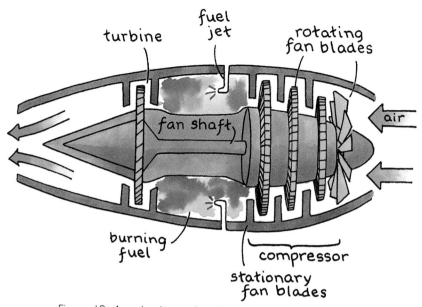

Figure 19. A turbo jet engine like the one drawn here provides the power for large passenger airplanes.

its pressure. The hot, pressurized gases pass through turbines that are used to turn the compressors and the intake fan. The gases then pass through the exhaust. Again, the plane's forward propulsion is explained by Newton's third law of motion—the gases pushed out the jet engine's exhaust exert an equal thrust forward on the plane.

ACTIVITY 17

A WATER HOSE JET

MATERIALS
- *water hose and nozzle*
- *string*
- *clothesline or suitable substitute from which to hang the water hose*

The principle that explains the motion of a jet-powered airplane (Newton's third law) can be seen when water emerges from a hose. Adjust the nozzle on a water hose until you have the most far-reaching stream possible. Then turn off the water and suspend the nozzle end of the hose from a clothesline or something similar as shown in Figure 20. Now, watch the nozzle closely as a friend turns on the faucet to which the hose is connected. Which way did the hose and nozzle move relative to the direction of the emerging water jet? How is this similar to the effect on a jet airplane when hot gases pass through its exhaust? What happens when the water is turned off?

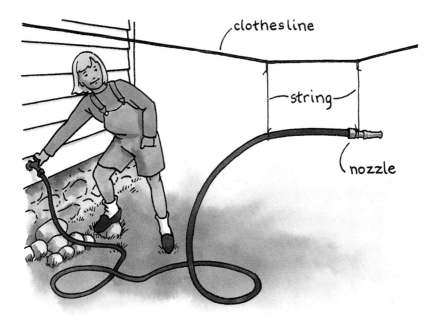

Figure 20. A water hose will illustrate the action of a jet engine when water emerges from the hose.

The speed of sound is about 1,200 km/hr (750 mi/hr). Today's fastest passenger airplanes travel at twice the speed of sound (Mach 2). They are not allowed to fly at supersonic speeds over land because they produce sonic booms that can shake buildings, break windows, and scare people. Airplanes traveling faster than the sound waves they produce create a cone-shaped pattern of overlapping sound waves as shown in Figure 21. The sound along the edges of the cone is very intense because, as you can see from the drawing, many sound waves come together there. When the edge of the cone reaches the ground, a very loud noise—sonic boom—is heard, which can damage buildings.

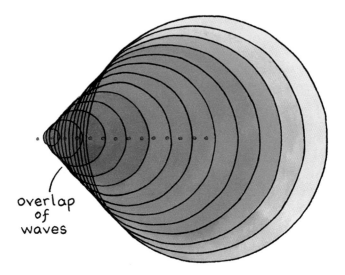

overlap
of
waves

Figure 21. The cone-shaped shock wave produced by a supersonic plane is shown in the drawing. The dots mark the position of the plane after equal periods of time as it moves from right to left. The dots are also the centers of the circular sound waves shown in the drawing that are produced by the plane. Notice that the last dot on the left, which marks the present position of the plane as it produces a new sound wave, is beyond the last wave it produced. The overlapping waves give rise to the loud sonic boom.

The supersonic *Concorde* is easily recognized by its needle
nose.

A similar effect is seen when a boat exceeds the speed of water waves. The wake produced corresponds to the cone-shaped sound waves seen in Figure 21.

Even at speeds of 2,400 km/hr (1,500 mi/hr), it takes 8.5 hours to travel halfway around the earth. Research has shown that people prefer trips that last no longer than two hours. To reduce earth's longest trip to two hours requires speeds of 9,600 km/hr (6,000 mi/hr)—eight times the speed of sound (Mach 8). Speeds in excess of five times the speed of sound (Mach 5) are said to be hypersonic. One hypersonic aircraft that has been proposed uses both jet and

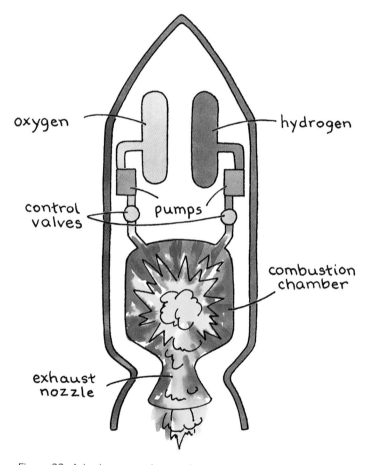

Figure 22. A hydrogen rocket carries its own oxygen because there is no air in space above the earth's atmosphere.

rocket engines. The jet engines would be used to take off and land and to carry the plane to altitudes of about 13 km (8 mi). At higher altitudes, where there is not sufficient air to power a jet, the plane would use rocket engines. Rocket engines carry their own oxygen and can, therefore, provide power in the airless space above the earth's atmosphere. For example, a hydrogen-powered rocket such as the one drawn in Figure 22 carries the liquid oxygen needed to burn the hydrogen that it also carries.

Another hypersonic plane that has been proposed will travel at speeds 25 times that of sound (Mach 25 or 28,800 km/hr [18,000 mi/hr]) so that it can go into orbit. Such a plane, which would be able to take off and land using jet engines, would replace the space shuttle. It could carry people and materials from earth to orbit and back again. Both these hypersonic planes would have to be made from special materials to withstand the 3,000°F (1,600°C) temperatures developed during high-speed reentry into the earth's atmosphere.

GOING FURTHER

In this book you have seen only a small portion of the science and technology of transportation. There is much more that you can investigate. A few of the things you might like to investigate are listed below.

★ • Use a tape measure, a ruler, and a yardstick or a meter stick to measure the diameter of a wheel. Then measure its circumference by wrapping the measuring tape or string around the wheel or by rolling the wheel through one turn as described in Activity 3. Do this for a number of wheels of different sizes and for other round things such as tin cans, cake pans, washers, and so on. Record the name of each circular object or wheel and its circumference and diameter in a data table. Divide the circumference of each round object or wheel by its diameter. What do you notice about the ratio: circumference/diameter? Can you predict the diameter of another round object by measuring its circumference? Does the relationship you have found hold true for spherical objects such as basketballs or soccer balls? How can you find out?

★ • Does a wheel really move in a circle when it turns? To find out, you can map the path of a point near a wheel's rim. Tape a marking pen to the rim of one of the rear wheels of a tricycle. Tape a long sheet of wrapping paper to a basement or garage wall or to a board fence. Then slowly roll the tricycle wheel along next to the paper. The pen will map the path followed by the wheel's rim on the paper. Does a rolling wheel move in a circle? If not, what kind of path does it follow? What is the path of a point at the center of a wheel?

★ • Draw a number of different size gears on sheets of cardboard. Cut out the gears. Put pins through their centers to mount them on larger sheets of cardboard. Arrange the gears so that their cogs meet. For two meshed gears, how are the diameters of the gears related to the number of times the second gear turns when the first one turns once? How can gears be used to change the direction that wheels turn?

★ • What is a worm gear? Where can you find such gears? Build a model to show how a worm gear works.

★ • A car's differential are the gears that allow the drive wheels on an automobile to turn at different speeds. See if you can find out how a differential works.

★ • Cars, like bicycles, use different gear ratios. Find out how gear ratios are changed in cars. Big trucks usually have many possible gear ratios. Can you explain why?

★ • Cars have a reverse gear—one that allows them to move backwards. How does this gear change the direction that the car moves? Other than its awkwardness, what prevents you from pedaling your bicycle backwards?

✖★ • Hero of Alexandria, an early Greek inventor, is usually credited with building the first steam engine. How did his engine work? With an adult to help you, can you build an engine similar to Hero's?

★ • An object placed in water is buoyed upward by a force equal to the weight of the liquid displaced. Does this law hold for other liquids as well? You might try rubbing alcohol, a solution of Epsom salts, mineral oil, and witch hazel.

★ • Build a model steam turbine. One such model is described in *The Thomas Edison Book of Easy and Incredible Experiments* (Wiley, 1988).

★ • Build a model sailboat. It's easy to see how a sailboat can move with the wind, but how can such boats travel into the wind?

★ • Although the basic ingredients of today's automobile were developed by 1900, the last century has seen many improvements in the auto industry. For example, modern cars have lights, electric starters, pneumatic, tubeless tires, automatic transmissions, fuel injectors, and so on. What other innovations have taken place in automobiles? Choose several of them and explain how they work.

GLOSSARY

Archimedes' principle: the buoyant force on an object in a fluid is equal to the weight of the fluid displaced by the object; consequently, the weight lost by such an object is equal to the weight of the fluid it displaces.

axle: a rod that connects two or more wheels on opposite sides of a vehicle.

Boyle's law: at constant temperature, the volume of an enclosed gas is inversely proportional to the pressure; that is, doubling the pressure on the gas will halve its volume.

Charles's law: at a fixed pressure, the volume of a gas increases uniformly with temperature; that is, if the volume of a gas increases by $\frac{1}{100}$ of its initial volume when the temperature rises one degree, its volume will grow by $\frac{1}{10}$ when the temperature rises ten degrees.

clutch: a device found in cars that consists of two plates, one attached to the flywheel, the other to the main shaft of the gearbox. When engaged, the clutch connects the turning flywheel to drive gears leading to a vehicle's wheels. When the clutch is disengaged, the motor can run and the flywheel turn without the car moving.

condenser: a device in which a gas, such as steam, is cooled so that it changes to a liquid, such as water.

differential: a set of gears that enables an engine to drive two wheels on opposite sides of a vehicle while allowing one wheel to turn faster than the other.

dirigibles (zeppelins): lighter-than-air ships made by covering a light aluminum frame with a thin material and filling the enclosed space with a gas such as hydrogen or helium. Propellers, powered by internal combustion engines, enable these ships to move in any direction through the air.

drag: friction due to motion through air. The frictional force acts in a direction that opposes the motion of the object.

flywheel: a large, heavy gear at the end of an engine's crankshaft. It smooths out the jerky motion of the pistons that drive the crankshaft.

friction: the force that opposes the motion of one surface as it slides over another.

front-wheel drive: a car in which the force generated by the engine is applied to the front wheels.

fusion (of hydrogen): the union of the nuclei of hydrogen atoms to form helium nuclei. The reaction, which releases vast amounts of energy per mass of helium formed, occurs only at very high temperatures such as those found in stars.

gear: a toothed wheel that meshes with another toothed element to transmit a motion or to change a speed or direction.

gravity: the force of attraction between two masses. The earth, for example, exerts a force on you that pulls you toward its center. You, in turn, exert an equal force on the earth (the third law of motion).

hypersonic: speeds greater than Mach 5.

inertia: the resistance to a change in motion. The greater an object's mass, the greater will be the force required to produce a given change in its motion.

internal combustion engine: an engine in which the fuel is burned within the engine's cylinders.

jet engines: engines that develop a forward thrust by drawing in air to burn a fuel, the gaseous products of which are ejected through a narrow exhaust nozzle. The gases pushed backward and out the jet engine's exhaust exert an equal push forward on the plane.

law of nature: a consistent regularity found in nature that can always be observed and predicted.

lever: a simple machine consisting of a rigid bar that turns on a fixed point (fulcrum) and can be used to change the direction and size of an applied force.

Mach number (Mach):: the ratio of the speed of an object to the speed of sound in the surrounding medium. An airplane moving through air with a velocity twice that of sound in air is said to be traveling at Mach 2.

magnetic levitation (maglev): a system that uses magnetic forces to lift a vehicle, such as a train, so that it floats, leaving a thin layer of air between track and train.

Newton's first law of motion: objects remain in motion or at rest unless acted on by outside forces.

Newton's second law of motion: an object accelerates in the direction of the force applied to it. The greater the force, the greater the acceleration; the larger the mass, the less the acceleration.

Newton's third law of motion: for every action force there is an equal but opposite reaction force. If someone pushes you to the right, you automatically push that person to the left.

odometer: a meter on a car or truck that tells you how far the vehicle has traveled. It consists of a series of gears and a flexible wire that connects a wheel to the meter.

piston: a solid cylinder in an engine that fits snugly into a larger hollow cylinder and moves back and forth under pressure changes created by steam, fluids, exploding vapors, etc.

port: the left side of a ship.

propeller: a series of blades mounted at the end of a shaft. Often the shaft is connected to an engine so that when the shaft turns, the blades push air or water in one direction and the vehicle is propelled in the opposite direction.

PRT (personal rapid transit): a computerized system consisting of small electrically powered vehicles moving along a lightweight, elevated track. By pressing a series of keys, a passenger can direct the vehicles to his or her desired destination along the shortest possible route.

ratio: one number divided by another (a fraction). For example, the ratio of the circumference of a circle to its diameter is π; that is,

$$\frac{\text{circumference}}{\text{diameter}} = \pi = 3.14$$

rear-wheel drive: a car in which the force generated by the engine is applied to the rear wheels.

sonic boom: supersonic airplanes, which travel faster than the sound waves they produce, create a cone-shaped pattern of overlapping sound waves. Sound along the edges of the cone is very intense because many sound waves come together there. When these edges of the cone reach the ground, a very loud noise—sonic boom—is produced.

spring scale: a calibrated spring used to measure forces.

starboard: the right side of a boat.

steam turbine: a machine that converts the energy of moving steam into rotational motion such as a spinning propeller.

UNITS AND THEIR ABBREVIATIONS

LENGTH

English	*Metric*
mile (mi)	kilometer (km)
yard (yd)	meter (m)
foot (ft)	centimeter (cm)
inch (in.)	millimeter (mm)

AREA

English	*Metric*
square mile (mi^2)	square kilometer (km^2)
square yard (yd^2)	square meter (m^2)
square foot (ft^2)	square centimeter (cm^2)
square inch (in.^{2})	square millimeter (mm^2)

VOLUME

English	*Metric*
cubic mile (mi^3)	cubic kilometer (km^3)
cubic yard (yd^3)	cubic meter (m^3)
cubic foot (ft^3)	cubic centimeter (cm^3)
cubic inch (in.^{3})	cubic millimeter (mm^3)
ounce (oz)	liter (L)
	milliliter (mL)

MASS

English	*Metric*
pound (lb)	kilogram (kg)
ounce (oz)	gram (g)

TIME
hour (hr)
minute (min)
second (s)

FORCE OR WEIGHT

English	*Metric*
ounce (oz)	newton (N)
pound (lb)	

SPEED OR VELOCITY

English	*Metric*
miles per hour (mi/hr)	kilometers per hour (km/hr)
miles per second (mi/s)	kilometers per second (km/s)
feet per second (ft/s)	meters per second (m/s)
	centimeters per second (cm/s)

TEMPERATURE

English	*Metric*
degrees Fahrenheit (°F)	degrees Celsius (°C)

ENERGY
calorie (cal)
Calorie (Cal)
joule (J)

POWER
watt (W) = joule per second (J/s)

ELECTRICAL UNITS
volt (V)
ampere (A)

MATERIALS

balloon, helium filled, or mylar bag
bathroom scale
bicycle, multispeed
block, wooden
board, long and wide
brick
calculator
cardboard
ceramic ring magnets with holes
   through their centers
clay
clock
clothesline
cylindrical oatmeal box
drawing compass
drinking glass
electric fan
glass bottle with a narrow neck
gloves
heavy cans with narrow rims (unopened
   one-gallon cans of paint)
ice water
laboratory balance
long ribbon
marbles, 5 or 6 of same diameter
marking pen

measuring cup, pint size
measuring tape
metal rollers
meter stick
one-gallon metal can, clean and empty,
   with screw-on cap or rubber stopper
   that fits its opening
paper
paper clips
paper fasteners
pencil
rubber bands
ruler
saucepan
scissors
seesaw
small toy doll
spring balances
spring scale
stopwatch
stove or hot plate
straight pins
straws, paper and plastic
string
syringe, needleless
tape

thumbtacks
toy airplane with rubber-band-powered
  propeller
toy car
toy pinwheel on stick
wagon, large
washcloth
water

water hose and nozzle
weight
wooden block
wooden dowels
wooden stakes
wood glue
yardstick

INDEX

ABOUT THE AUTHOR

Robert Gardner, science educator and award-winning author of nonfiction for young people, has written over fifty books to introduce readers to the wonders of science. A *School Library Journal* reviewer has called him "the master of the science experiment book."

He earned a B.A. from Wesleyan University and an M.A. from Trinity College. Before retiring, he taught biology, chemistry, physics, and physical science for over thirty years at Salisbury School in Salisbury, Connecticut. He and his wife, Natalie, reside in Massachusetts where he serves as a consultant on science education and continues to write books for future scientists.